ALL PATHS LEAD TO BETHLEHEM

BY PATRICIA & FREDRICK MᶜKISSACK
ILLUSTRATED BY KATHRYN E. SHOEMAKER

*"But you, Bethlehem Ephrathah, though you are small
among the clans of Judah,
out of you will come for me one who will be ruler over Israel. . . ."*
—Micah 5:2

AUGSBURG Publishing House • Minneapolis

To Our Son, Fred McKissack

Scripture quotations unless otherwise noted are from the Holy Bible:
New International Version. Copyright 1978 by the New York International
Bible Society. Used by permission of Zondervan Bible Publishers.

LCCCN 87-070473   ISBN 0-8066-2265-2

Manufactured in the U.S.A.   AF 10-0220

It is almost Christmas—in Bethlehem and all over the world. In the country and in the city, high in snowy mountains and throughout dry, desert lands, along the seashores and in the hot, steamy rain forests, people are waiting for Christmas to come.

3

Far from the city, on a small farm in the Midwest, a father patiently untangles a string of many-colored lights. Snowflakes glisten in the morning sunlight as a boy playfully makes a snow-angel.

"Tell me again about the angel who came to the Virgin Mary," says the boy.

His father nods and continues to hang the lights across the porch. "The world had been waiting a long time for the Savior to come," he answers. "God decided it was time. He sent an angel with good news. Soon the long wait would be over."

The spicy smell of cinnamon and nutmeg coming from Apartment 3-C lets the neighbors know Christmas is coming to the city. A holly wreath surrounded by Christmas cards decorates their door.

A mother and daughter bake cookies in the familiar Christmas shapes—bells, stars, and candles. They hum "Silent Night, Holy Night" as they fill gift boxes to be delivered later.

The girl spreads sweet icing on a cookie-angel's wings. "Tell me again about the angel who came to the Virgin Mary," says the girl.

Her mother smiles. "The world had been waiting a long time for the Promised One to come," she says. "Finally, God sent the angel with good news to Mary. Soon the long wait would be over."

While they are waiting for Christmas to come, mothers and fathers all over the world tell their children about the angel's visit to Mary.

Mary was frightened when the angel of the Lord came to her. But the angel said, "Don't be afraid. You are blessed. God has chosen you to be the mother of his Son. And when the child is born you are to name him Jesus."

"How can this happen?" wondered Mary.

"God's Spirit will make it happen," answered the angel.

Then Mary said, "Let it be as God wants. I am happy to serve him." And the angel was gone. *(Luke 1:26-38)*

Christmastime in Ghana is the cocoa season—a time of great joy, a time to celebrate and give thanks.

A father and son walk home from the marketplace together. The boy sings, *"Egbona hee; egbona hee. Egogo vo!"*

"Just so. Just so," says the father. "Christ is coming. Christ is coming. He is near!"

In Ireland, a father and daughter walk home together after an evening of caroling.

"Why do we put lights in our windows?" asks the girl.

"To welcome and guide travelers, who, like Mary and Joseph, may be on a journey this night," answers the father.

"Why did Mary and Joseph go to Bethlehem?"

"It was the order of Caesar Augustus," says the father. "And it was near the time for the babe to be born."

It is almost Christmas, and all over the world children are listening to their fathers tell about Mary's and Joseph's journey to Bethlehem.

Caesar Augustus ordered that every man, woman, and child he ruled had to be counted. Mary and Joseph lived in Nazareth, but they had to be counted in Joseph's hometown, Bethlehem. They had to travel over steep and rocky paths. When they arrived in Bethlehem, it was very near the time for Jesus to be born. *(Luke 2:1-5)*

It is the day before Christmas in Germany. A brother and sister wait upstairs for the *Mutter* to finish decorating the *Christbaum*, the Christ Child Tree. The *Vater* tells them a lovely story while they wait.

"A poor woodcutter and his wife welcomed a cold and hungry boy into their home. They did not know it was the Christ child they were helping," says the father. "As a gift for their special kindness, the child blessed the fir tree. So, the *Christbaum* reminds us to be loving and caring."

Mother calls, and the children hurry down the steps to see the huge evergreen, decorated with twinkling lights, brightly colored glass balls, strings of cookies, and shimmering tinsel.

"We are like the woodcutter and his wife," says the girl. "We make room in our house and hearts for the Christ child."

Christmas Eve comes to a family in Mexico. A brother and sister wait for their guests. A group of friends and neighbors, dressed in brightly colored fiesta clothes, gather outside the house. They carry lighted candles. The last night of the *Posada* celebrations is about to begin.

"Is there room for us?" the guests ask.

"Yes," answers the boy. "There is room in our house for the holy family."

The guests come inside. The house is decorated with Spanish moss, garlands of evergreen, colored paper lanterns, candles, and an altar with the *Nativity.* The brother and sister lead the guests through the house. She sings a lullaby to baby Jesus. "We make room in our house and hearts for the Christ child," says the boy.

All over the world families are remembering to be sharing and caring and to welcome the Christ child into their homes and their hearts.

When Joseph and Mary came to Bethlehem there was no room in the inn for them to stay. Joseph found a place for them in a stable where the animals slept. It wasn't as nice as the inn, but it was warm, and Joseph made a bed of hay for Mary to lie down in. *(Luke 2:7)*

14

Christmas is coming to Spain. A small girl helps her grandmother unpack the beautifully handcarved statues of Mary and Joseph from the old cedar trunk. The statues have been in the family for as long as anyone can remember. Carefully the girl places them in the little wooden stable. "*Abuela, Noche Buena,*" says the girl.

"Christmas Eve is The Good Night," says the grandmother. And they sing a very old carol.

In Italy, a small boy holds his grandmother's frail hand as they move slowly along. The narrow path winds upward into the hills outside their village.

On the hilltop, the two pilgrims are greeted by family and neighbors who have come to light their candles, sing, and pray before the living *presepio* scene.

"*Nonna*, is this the way it was so long ago in Bethlehem?"

"*Si, Nipotino*," says the grandmother. "Our Lord was born in a lowly stable."

On Christmas Eve, grandmothers in many nations and in many languages tell their grandchildren about the miracle of Jesus' birth.

Just as God planned, Jesus was born in a stable with a lamb, an ox, and a donkey looking on. Mary wrapped the newborn baby in strips of cloth. "Jesus is his name," she said, and she placed him in a manger. *(Luke 2:6-7)*

On Christmas Eve in France, children go from house to house, singing the good news the angels brought the shepherds: "Unto you a Savior has been born."

Afterward the children hurry home to warm their feet beside a burning Yule log and set their shoes by the fireplace in hopes that *Le Petit Jesus* will leave them a treat.

In Australia, on Christmas Eve, it is summer. Sail boats bob up and down on a calm ocean.

"Will Jesus hear us singing here in Australia?" asks a little girl.

"He will hear," answers her teacher. "Your voices are as lovely as the angels who brought the good news to the shepherds on that faraway hillside, long ago in Bethlehem."

The girl happily takes her place among the hundreds of other school children who have gathered to sing carols on a hillside overlooking a white, sandy beach and crystal blue water.

Hundreds of white doves are released, as the children joyfully sing, "Peace on earth, goodwill to men."

On Christmas Eve, millions of children everywhere share the message of the Christmas angels.

Outside the town of Bethlehem shepherds were watching their flocks. Suddenly, the sky was filled with light, and an angel came to them. "Don't be afraid. I bring you good news. A Savior has been born in Bethlehem. Go and find him lying in a manger," the angel said.

Then other angels came, and they sang, "Peace on earth to men of goodwill."

The shepherds rushed into the town and found baby Jesus lying in a manger. The shepherds thanked God for sending the Savior into the world. *(Luke 2:8-16)*

22

It is Christmas Eve in Japan. A small boy steps on stage holding a bright star above his head. The audience grows quiet.

"This is the star of Bethlehem," the boy says, smiling broadly. "It led the Wise Men to Jesus."

The boy looks for his parents in the audience. There they are. His parents smile. The boy bows. "*Meri Kurisumasu*," he says to the audience.

"*Meri Kurisumasu*," they respond.

In Sweden the night lights sparkle in an inky sky. The big Clydesdale impatiently stamps his hoof in the packed snow. The bells on his harness jingle. Twins, bundled in look-alike snowsuits, climb aboard the sleigh and snuggle against their mother. She wraps them in a woolen blanket. The father carries a torch as he guides the sleigh through the snowdrifts towering on each side of the road.

Outside the small church, friends and neighbors toss their torches into a heap. The flames leap high into the sky.

"It is as bright as the star the Wise Men followed," the children say.

"*Ja*," says the father. "When the Wise Men saw the great light in the heavens they followed it."

Christmas is coming, and in every part of the world, families tell the story of the Wise Men who came to see Jesus in Bethlehem.

In distant lands Wise Men saw a star brighter than any they had ever seen before. They followed the star to Bethlehem, where they found Jesus. The Wise Men gave Jesus gifts of gold, incense, and myrrh. They bowed down and worshiped him. *(Matthew 2:9-11)*

Christmas Eve comes to the Soviet Union. It is cold and snowy outside, but warm inside the small apartment.

A mother sets the Christmas table and hums a very old carol, "Christ the King of Glory Comes." The children help with the chores.

"Who is the extra plate for?" asks the youngest child.

"It is for those *whom nobody can see*," the mother answers. "People who are living in exile."

"Do you mean people who have been forced to leave their homes?" asks the oldest child.

The mother nods. "Yes. We set a place for them so they are not forgotten. When we worship in spirit and truth, they are with us."

"Jesus had to live in exile for a while," says the eldest child. "Tell us the story again, mother."

Christmas is coming very soon, and children all over the world wonder as they are told the story of Jesus' family's flight into Egypt.

One night after the Wise Men had left, an angel visited Joseph in a dream. God had sent the angel with a warning: "King Herod wants to kill Jesus. Take the mother and child to Egypt. You will be safe there."

Joseph obeyed the angel. Mary, Joseph, and Jesus lived in Egypt until King Herod died. Then God sent another angel to tell Joseph they could return home. So, Joseph took Mary and Jesus to live in Nazareth. It was the way God had planned. *(Matthew 2:13-23)*

It is late Christmas Eve high in the Swiss Alps. A boy sleepily follows his grandfather through the frosty night.

"Where do we go, grandpapa?" asks the boy.

"To Bethlehem," he answers.

"But we can't walk all the way to Bethlehem from Switzerland!"

"On Christmas Eve, all paths lead to Bethlehem," answers the old man.

At last they come to the village church. In the small tower bellroom, they warm themselves with a cup of steamy cocoa.

The minute and hour hands on the village clock jump to 12. The grandfather winks his eye, and the boy knows.

"I love you, grandpapa!" he exclaims. And, with a shout of joy and a big tug, the boy pulls the bell rope for the first time. In churches everywhere choirs sing, "Christ the Savior is born!"

It is Christmas day—in Bethlehem and all over the world!